Presenting:

BLUE HUE

A REVIEW OF THE COLOR BLUE!

**WORDS & ART BY:
BRIANNA DAVIS**

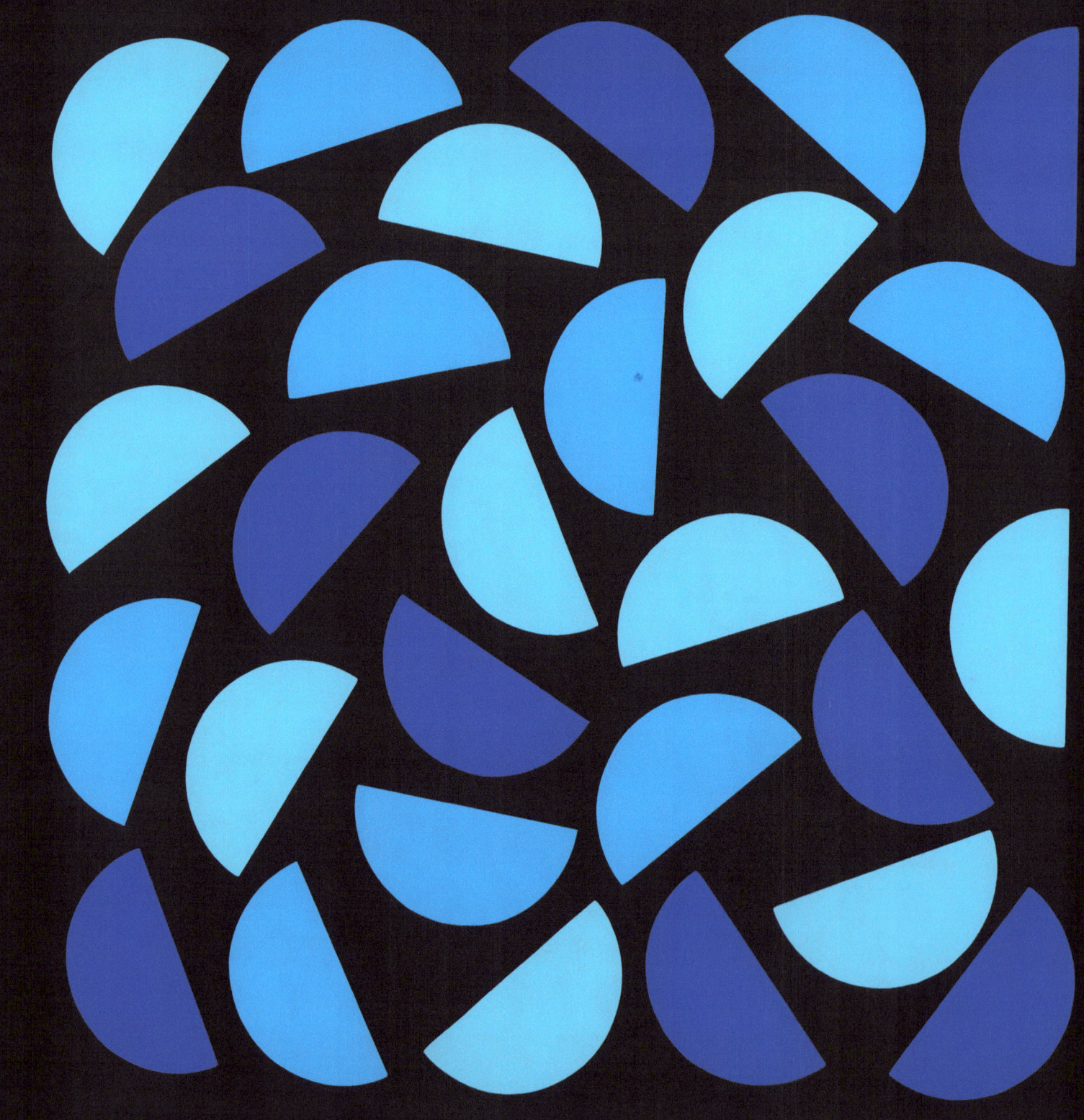

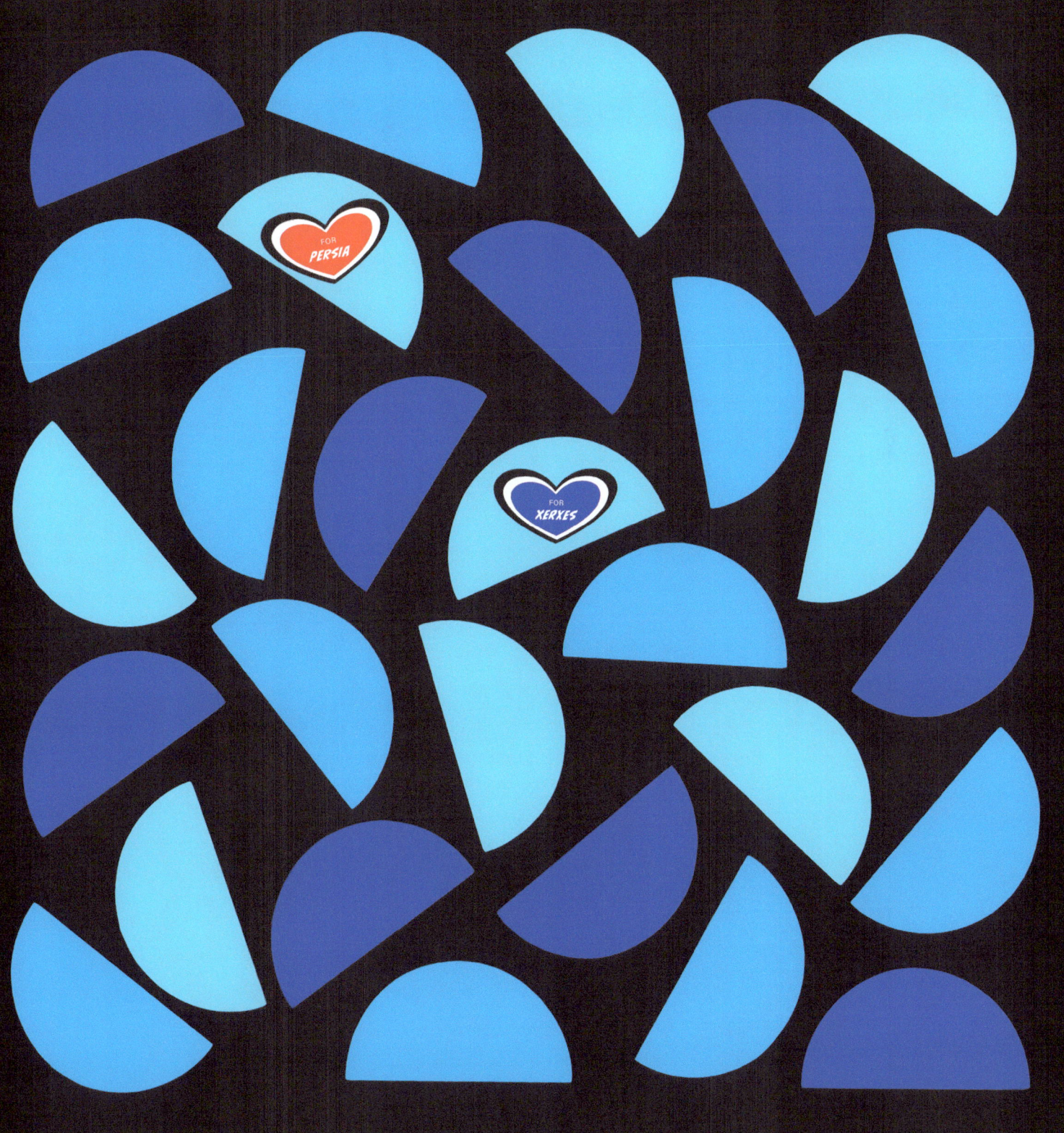

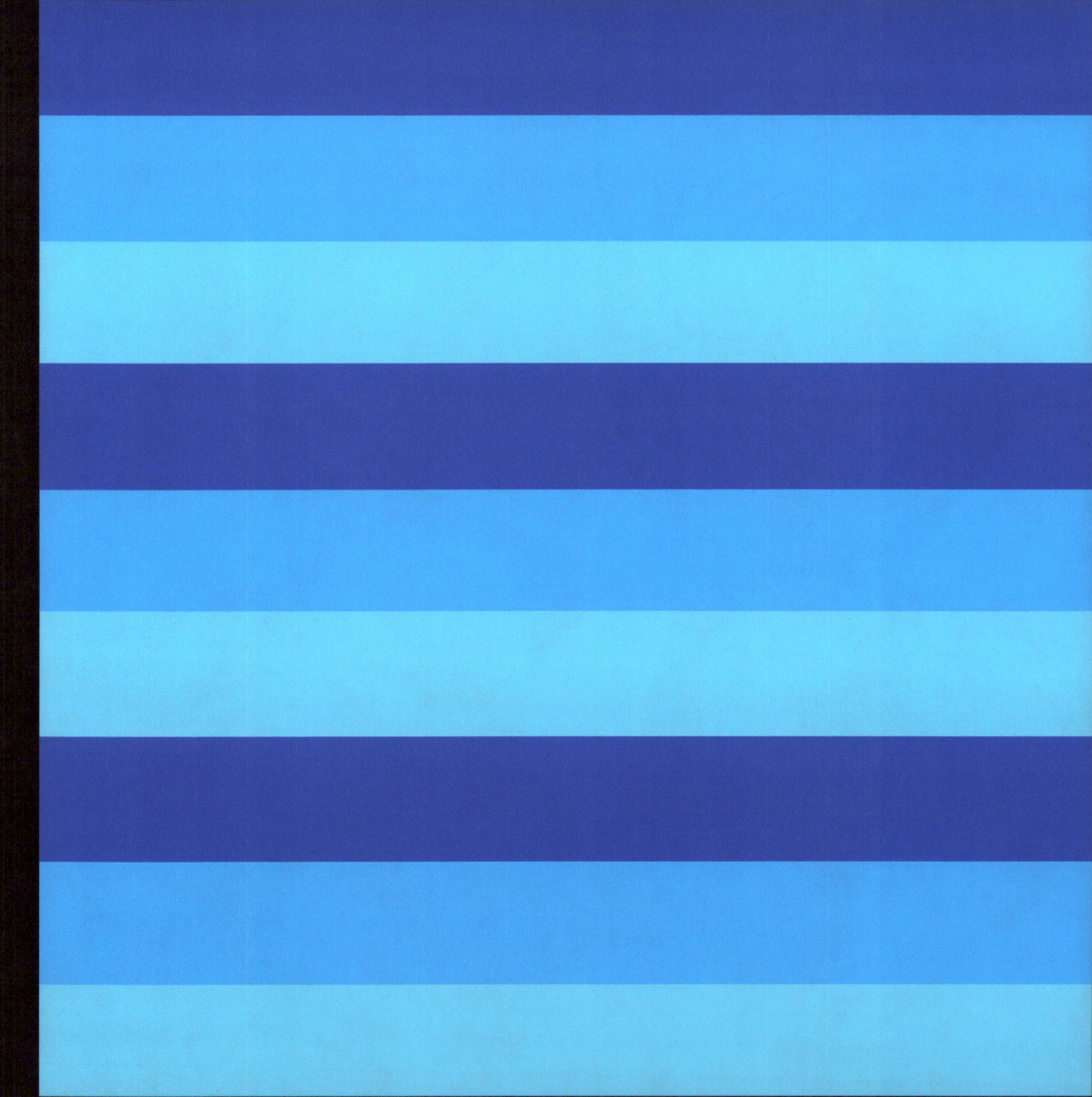

BLUE

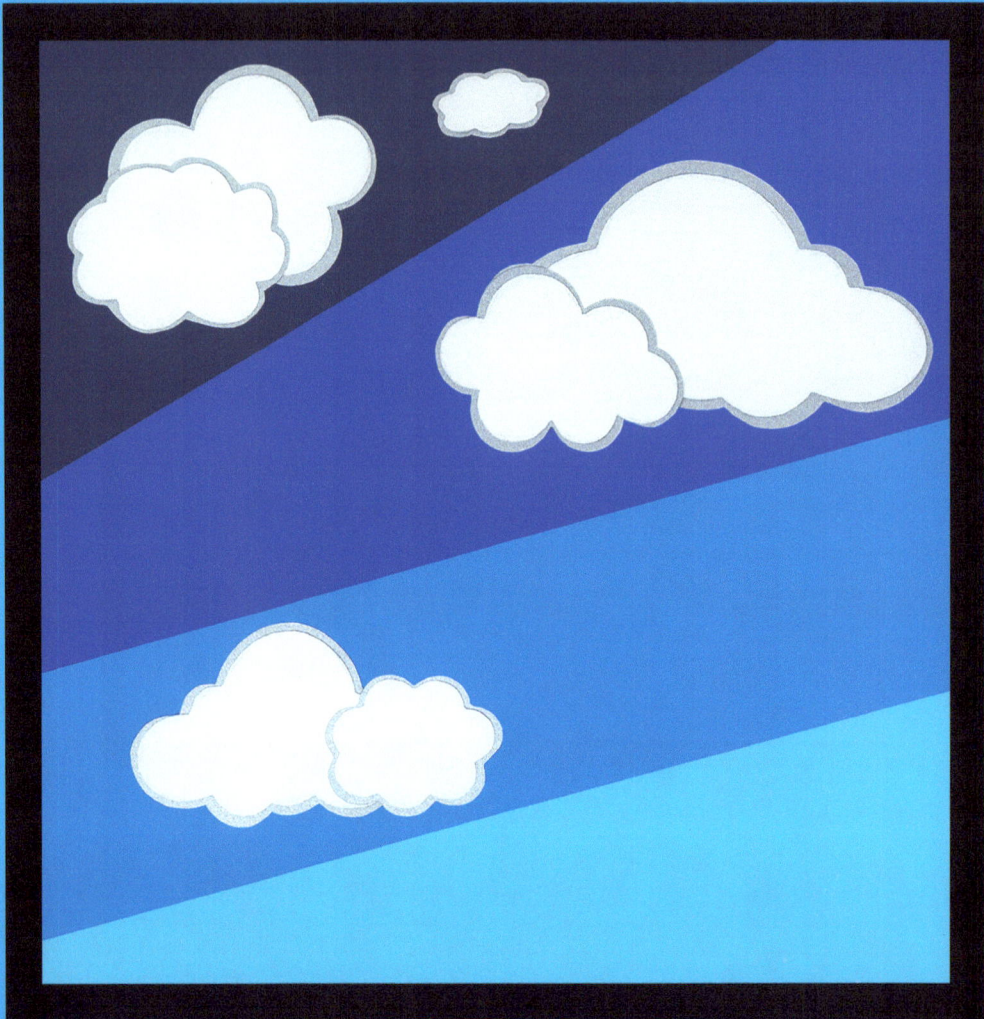

THE SKY IS A WONDERFUL THING THAT IS BLUE...

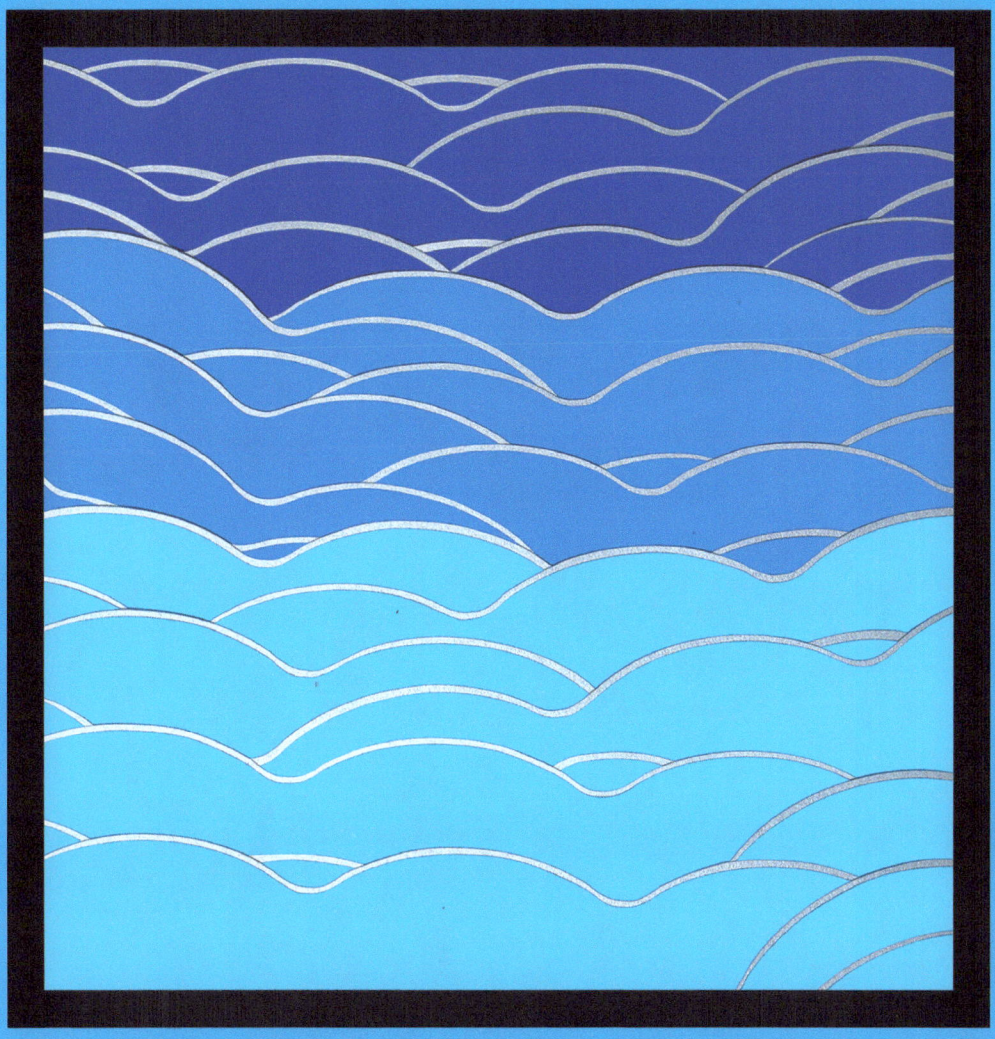

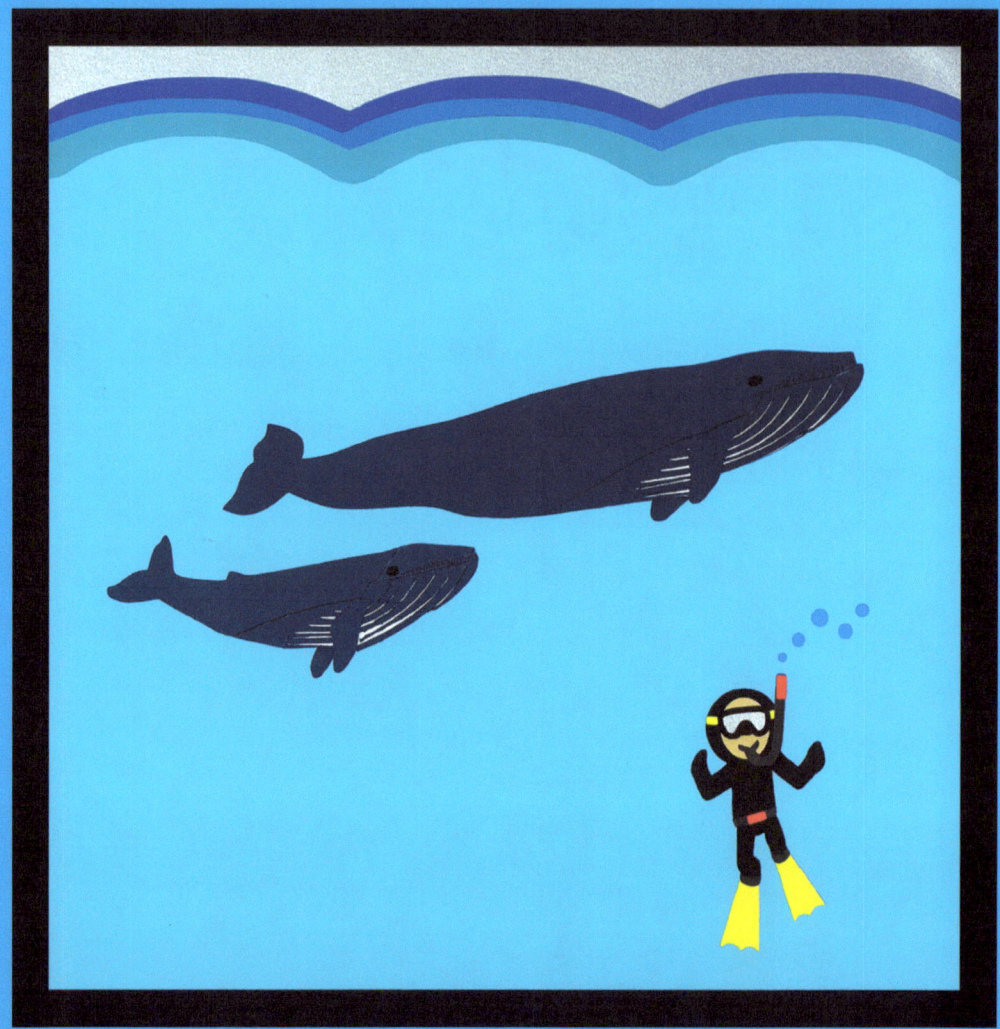

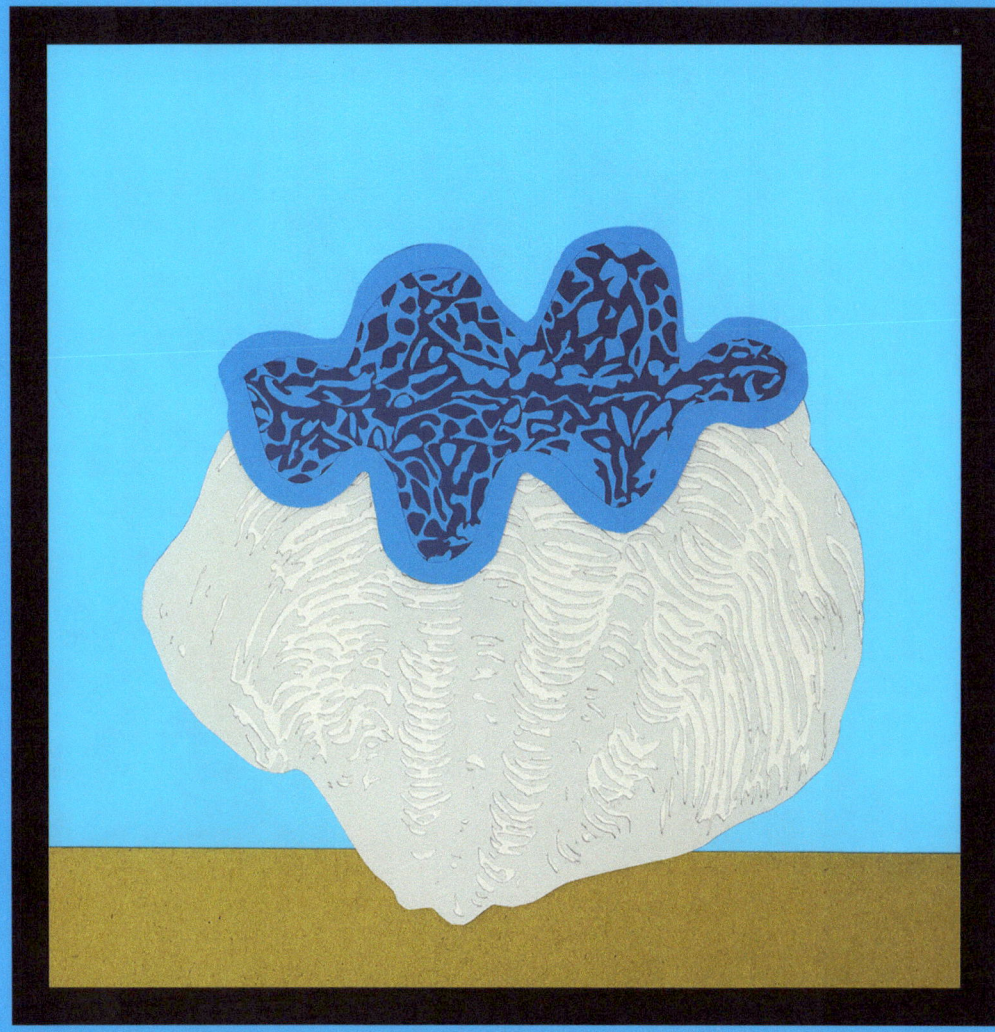

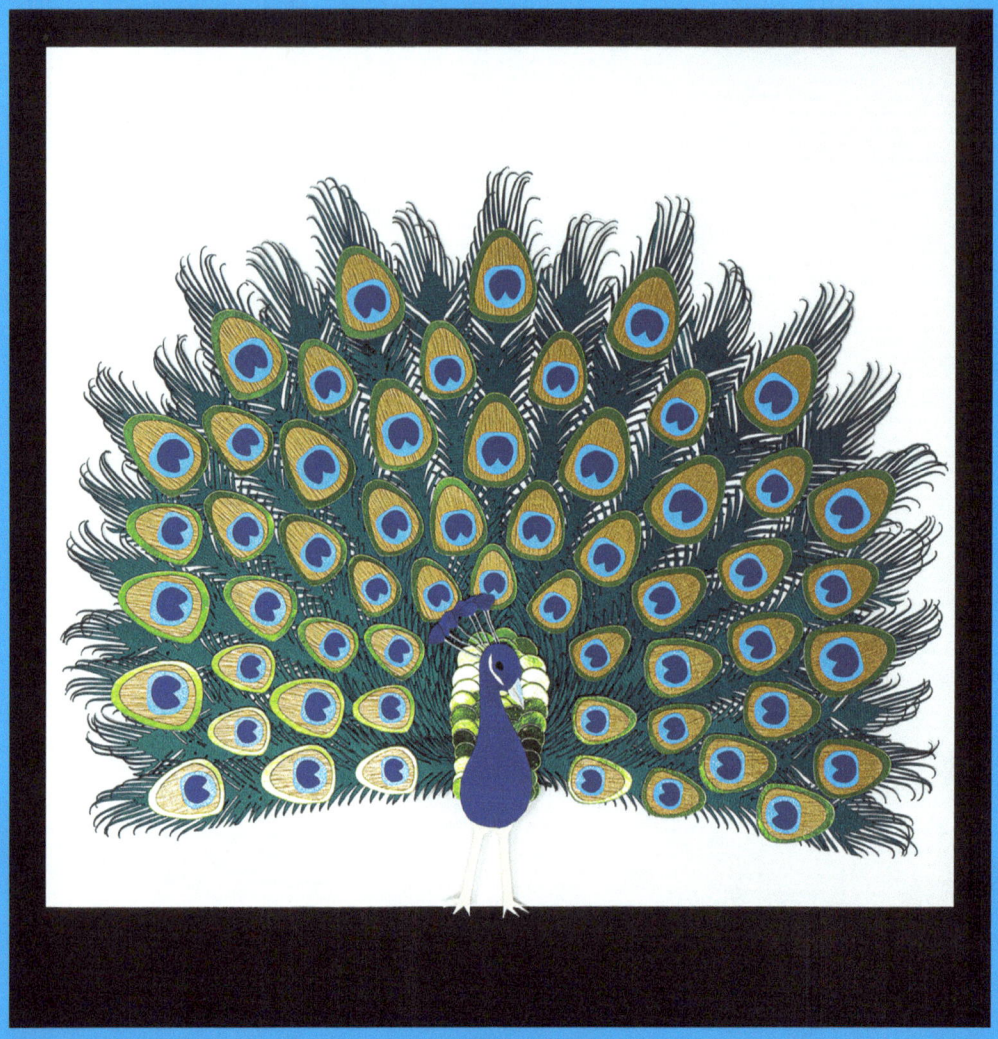

A PEACOCK HAS A BLUE BODY...

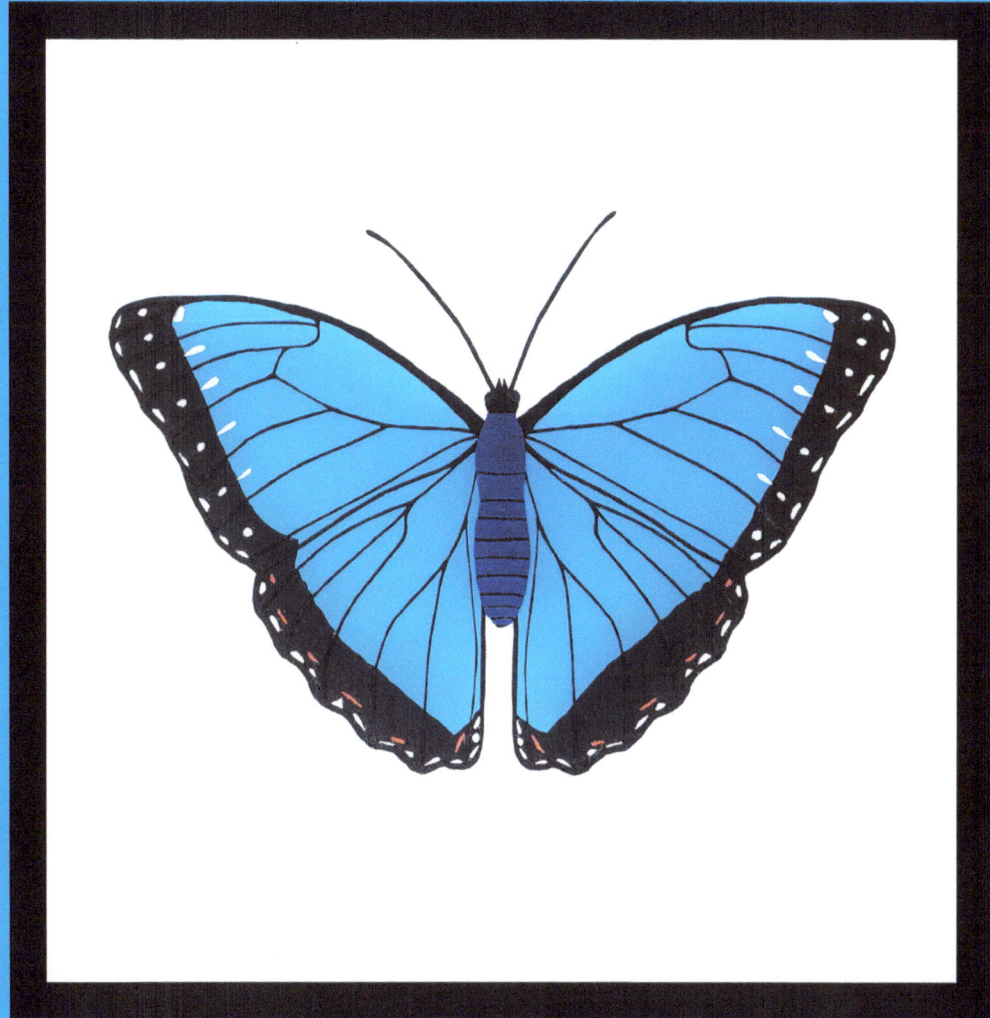

THE BLUE MORPHO BUTTERFLY IS SPOTTY!

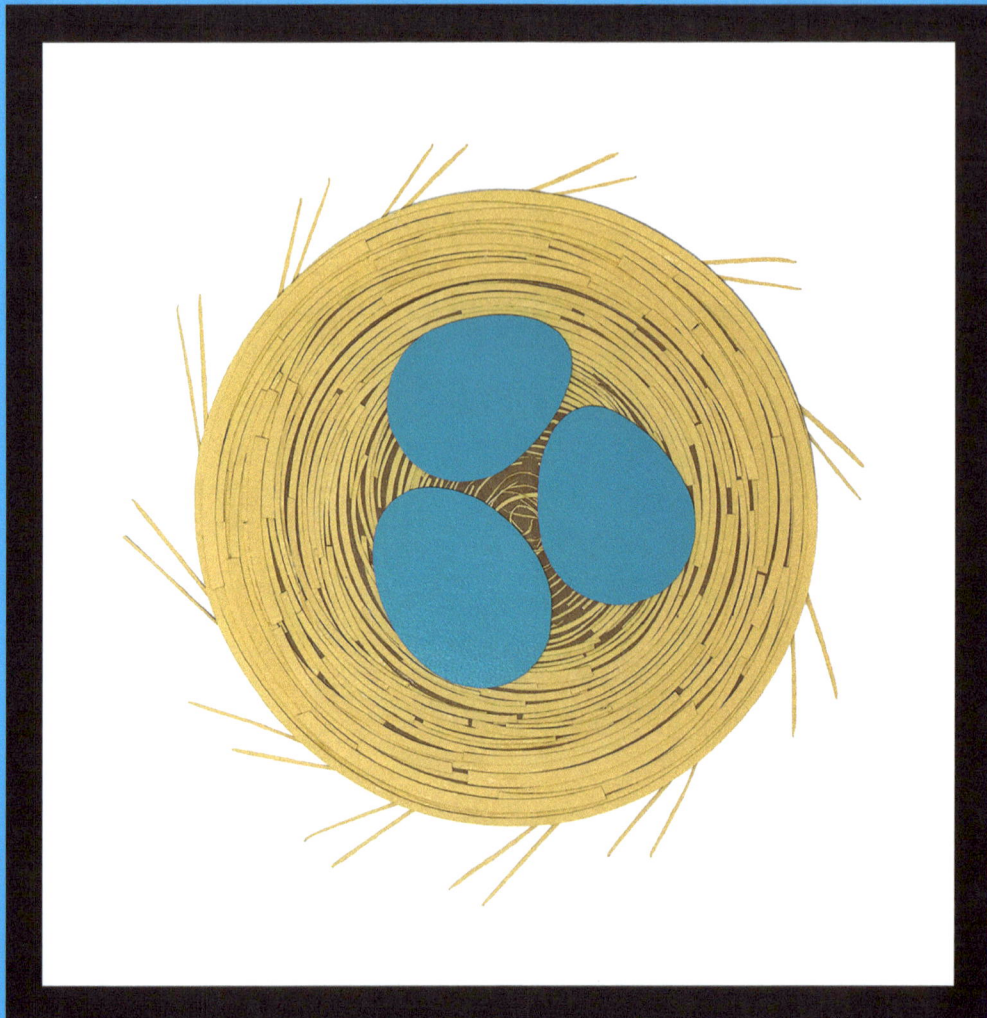

ROBIN'S EGGS ARE A VERY SPECIAL BLUE...

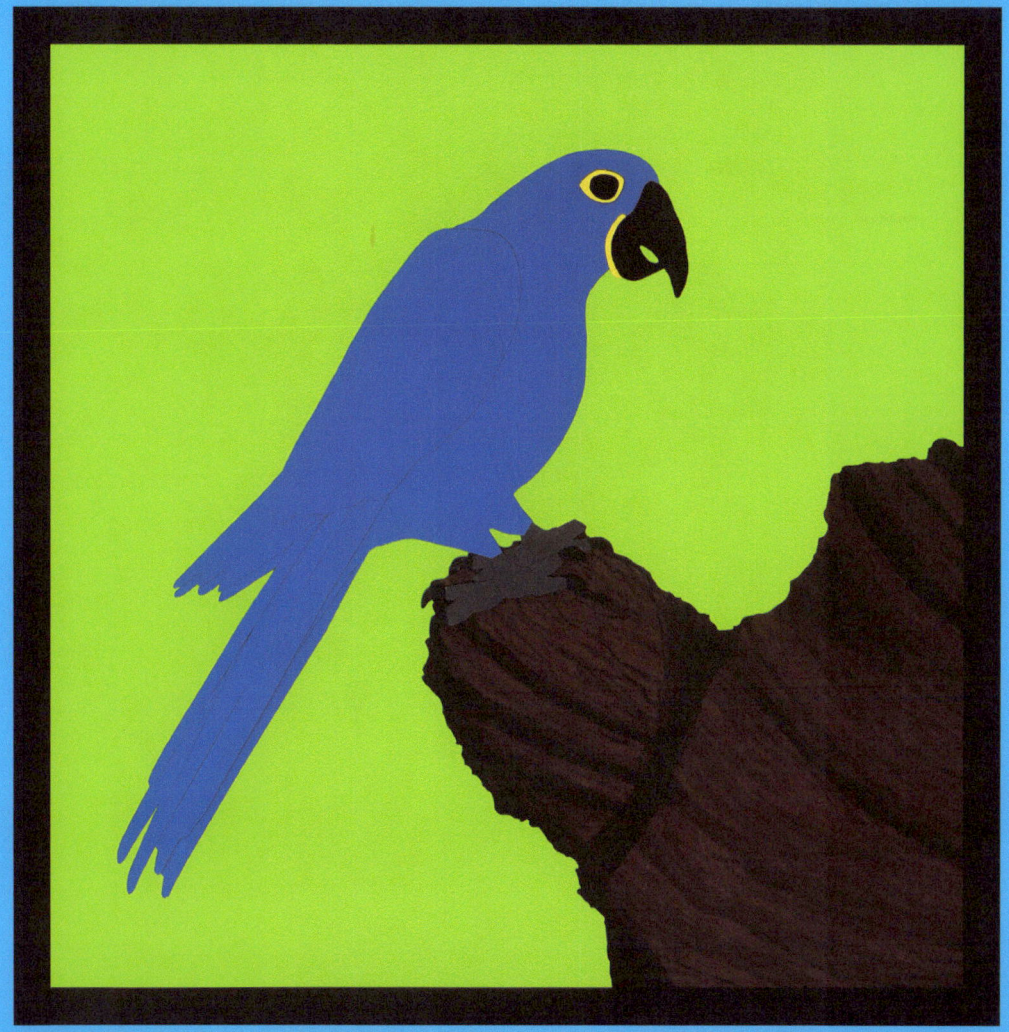

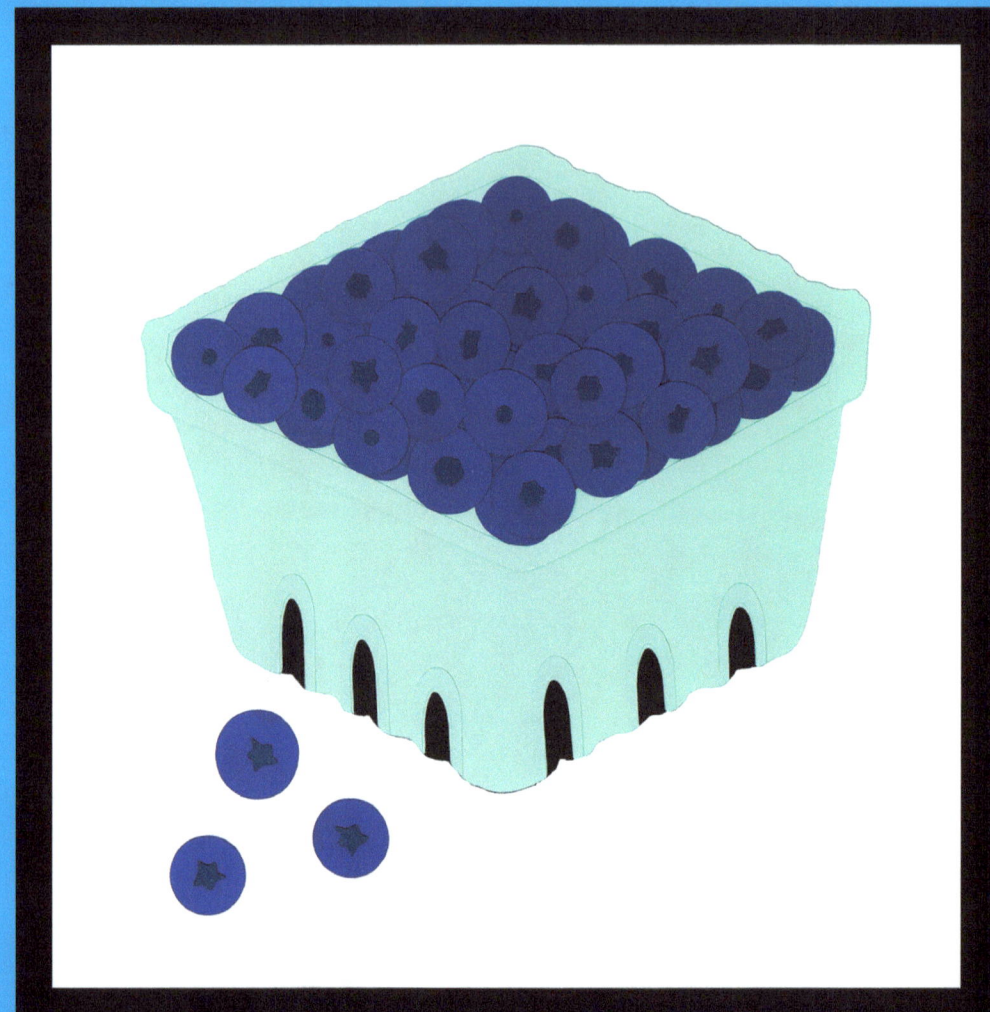

BLUEBERRIES ARE A POPULAR FRUIT...

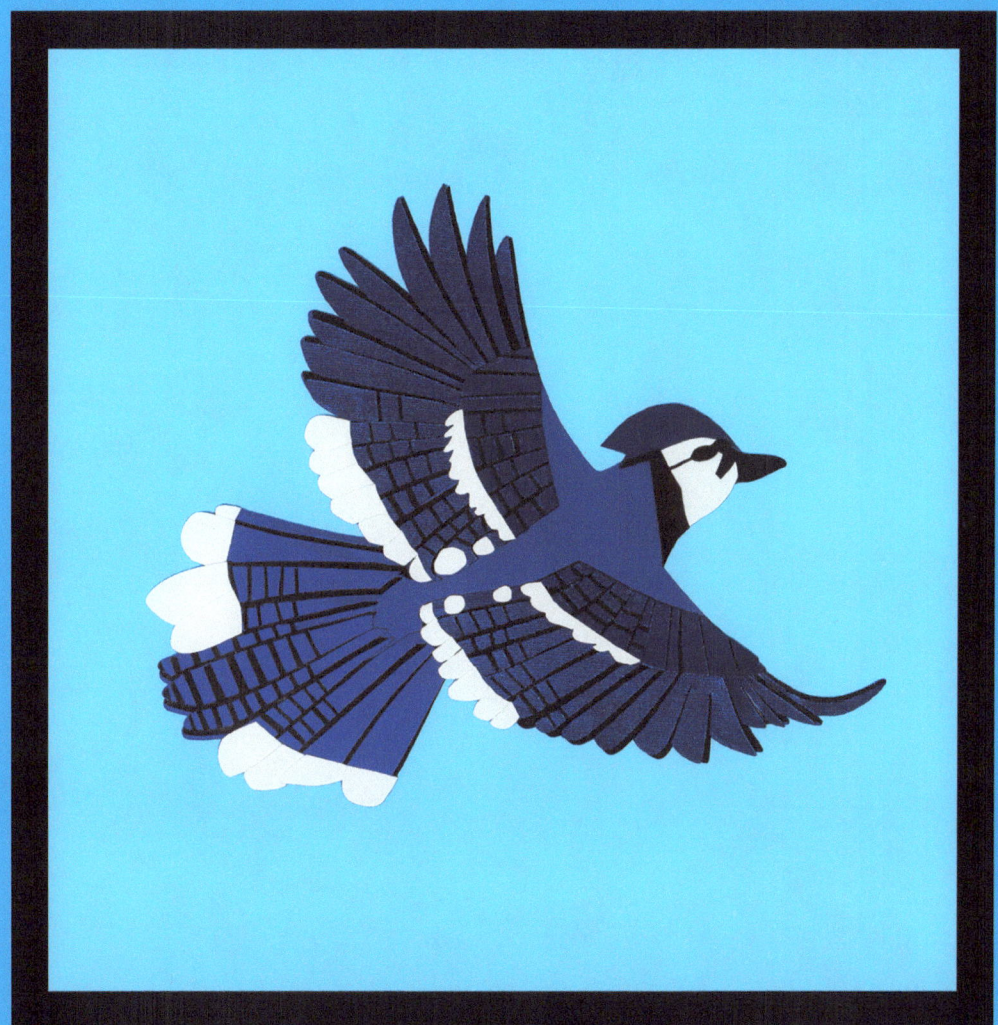

DO YOU SEE THE BLUE JAY EN ROUTE?

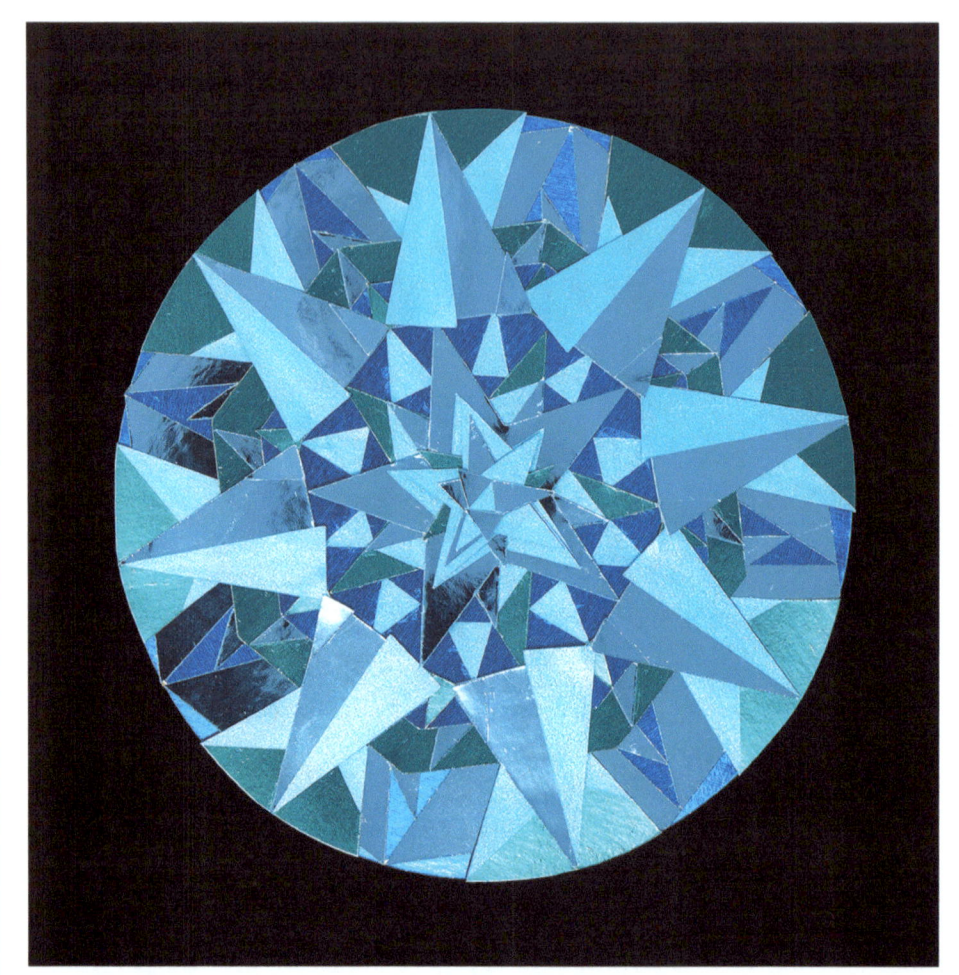

AQUAMARINE HAS A SHIMMERING GLEAM...

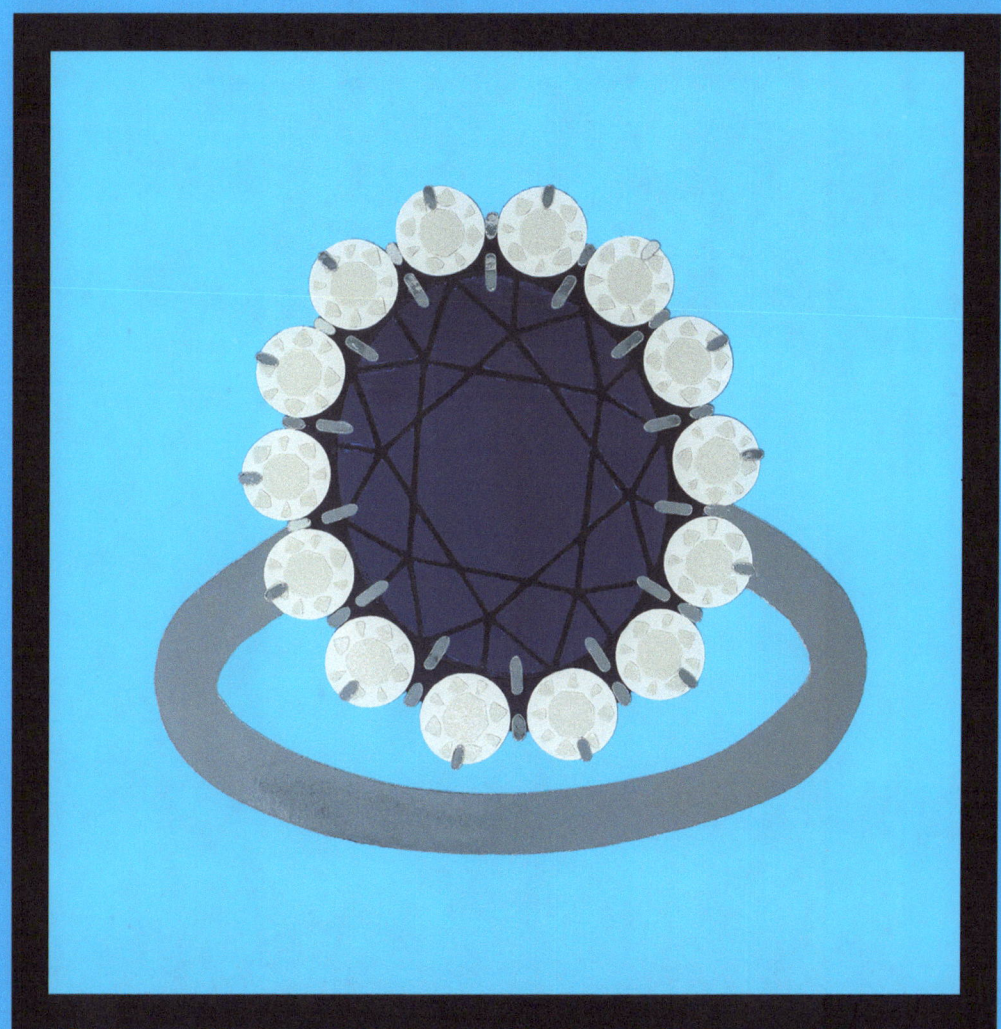

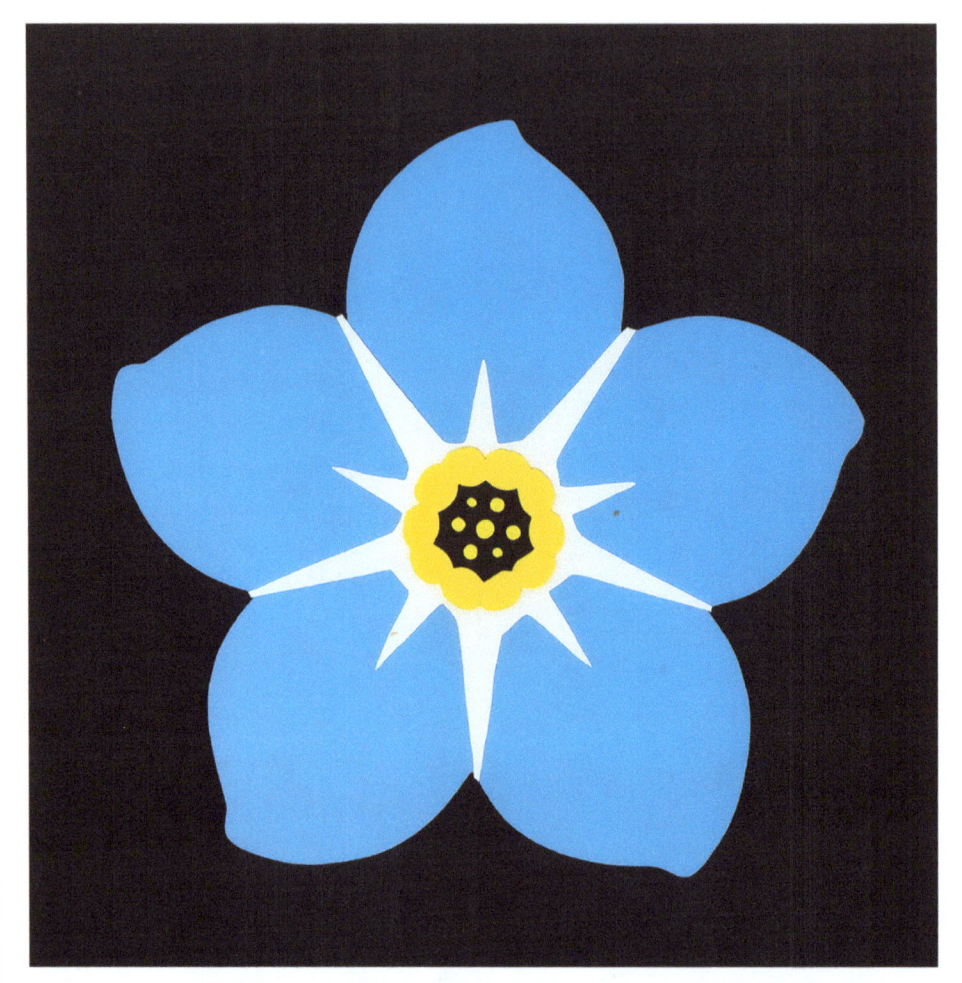

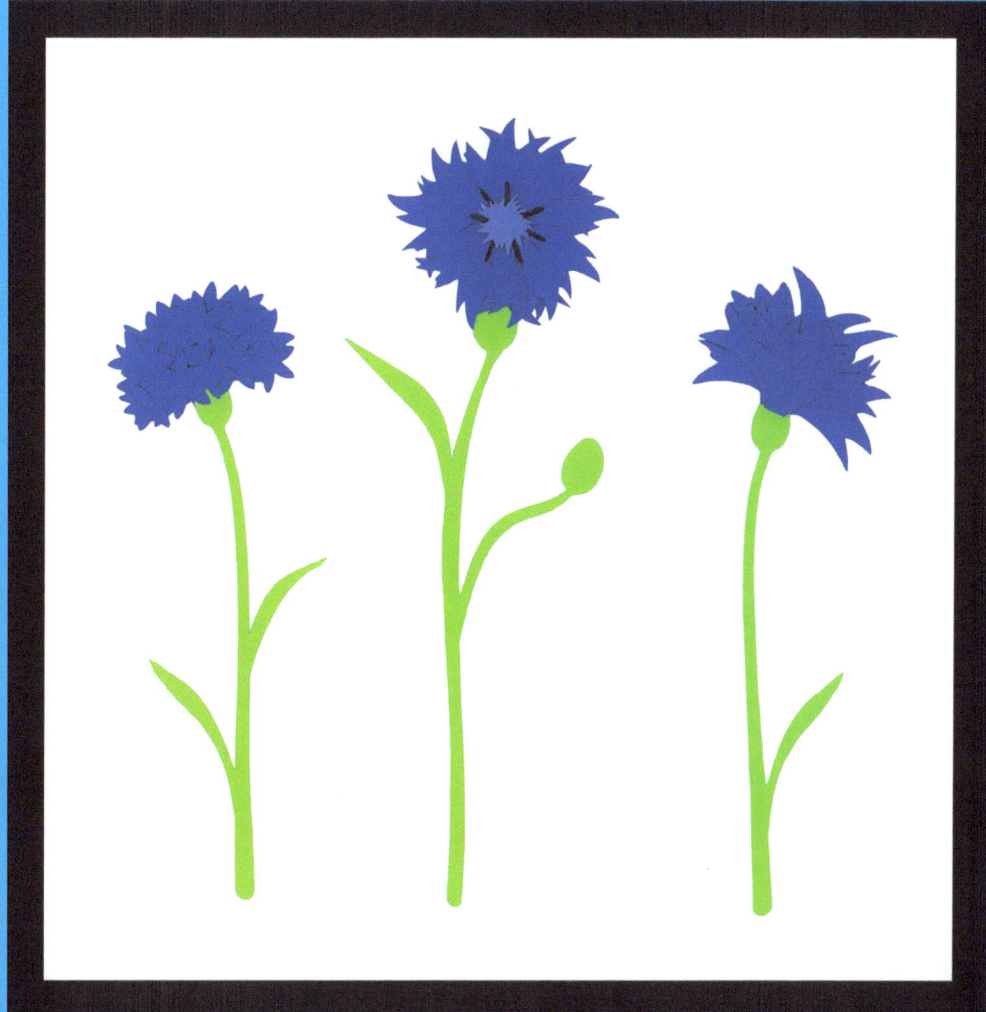

LET'S REVIEW EVERYTHING WITH A BLUE HUE!

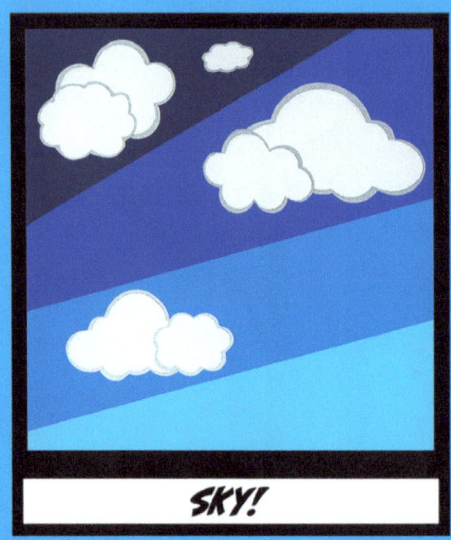
SKY!

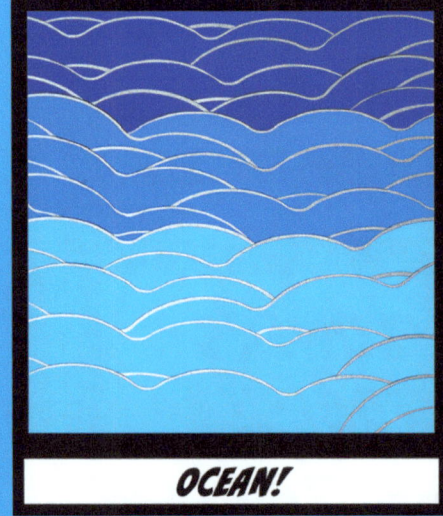
OCEAN!

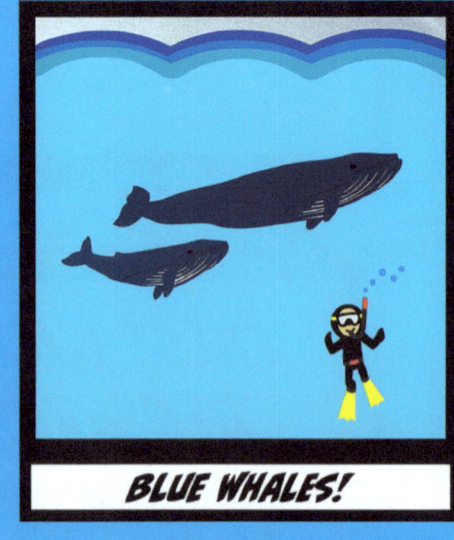
BLUE WHALES!

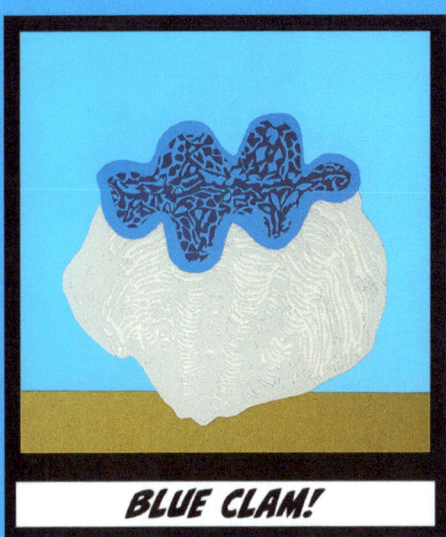
BLUE CLAM!

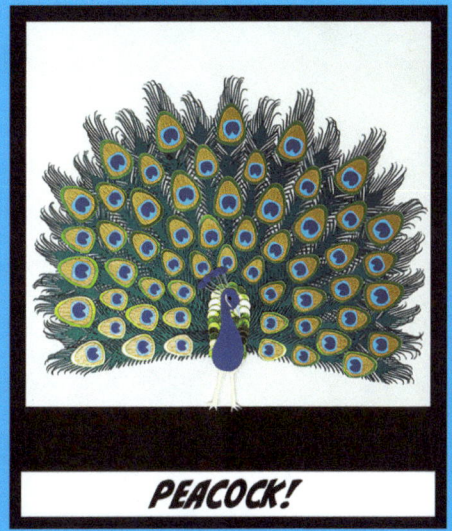
PEACOCK!

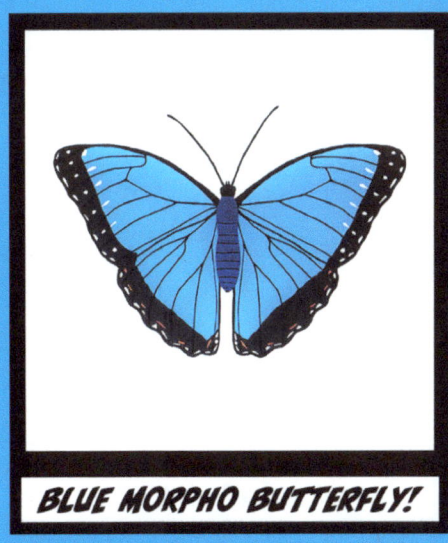
BLUE MORPHO BUTTERFLY!

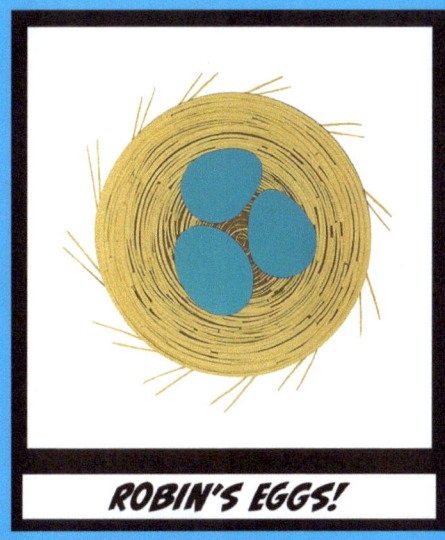
ROBIN'S EGGS!

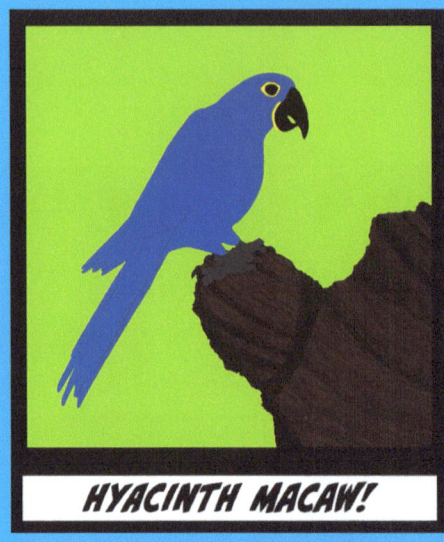
HYACINTH MACAW!

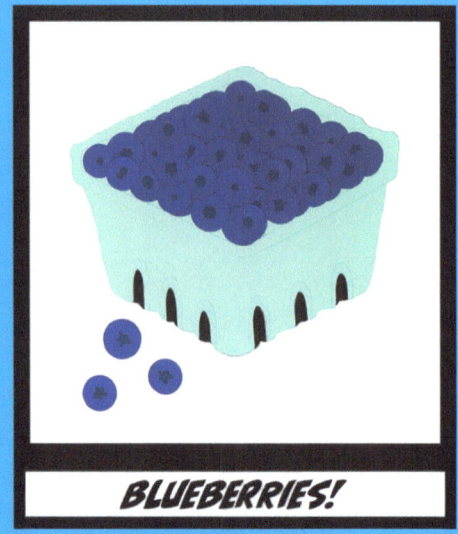
BLUEBERRIES!

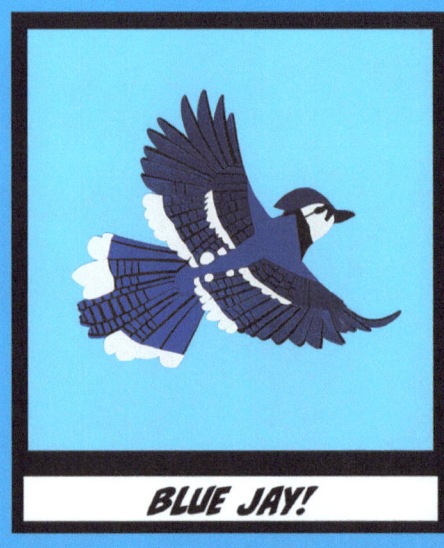
BLUE JAY!

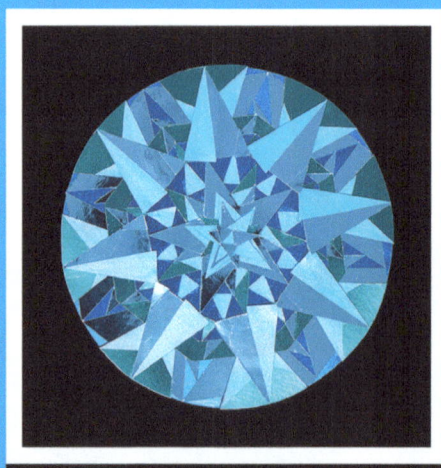
AQUAMARINE!

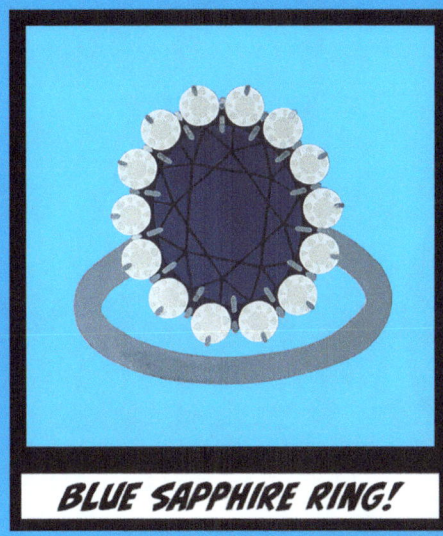
BLUE SAPPHIRE RING!

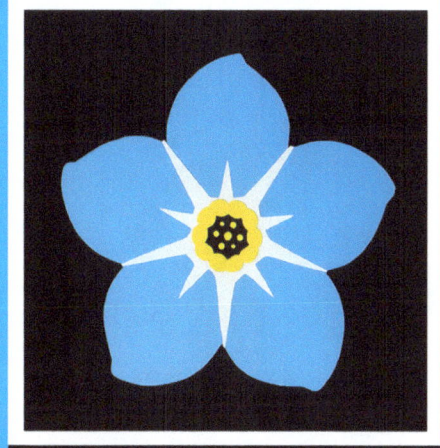
FORGET-ME-NOT FLOWER!

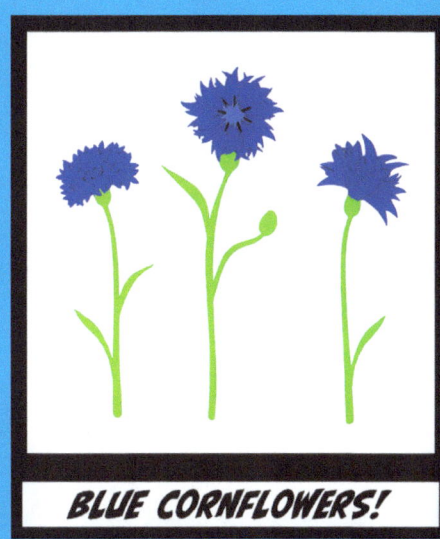
BLUE CORNFLOWERS!

NICE JOB, AND NOW WE'RE THROUGH. ISN'T IT FUN TO LEARN SOMETHING NEW!

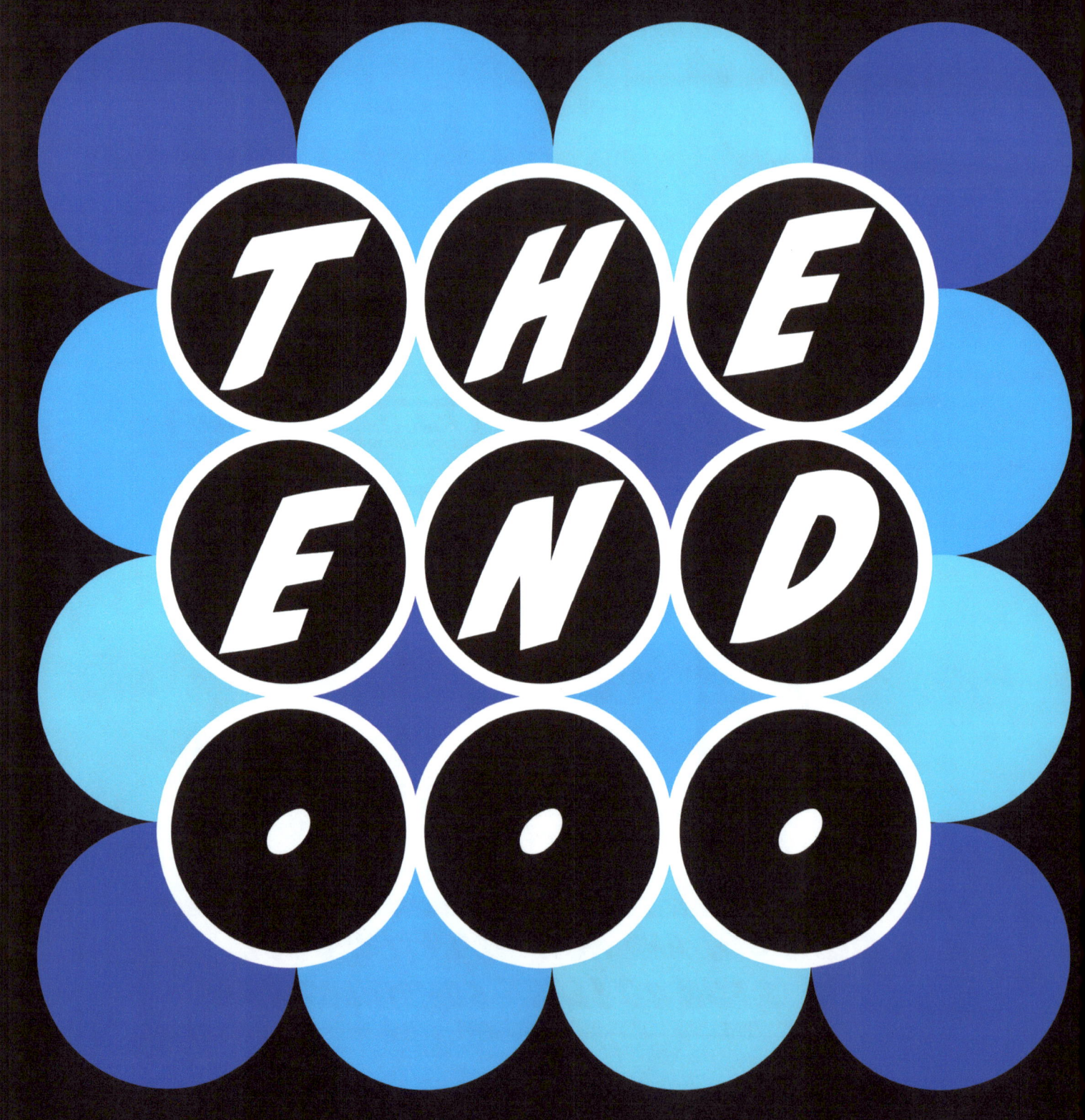

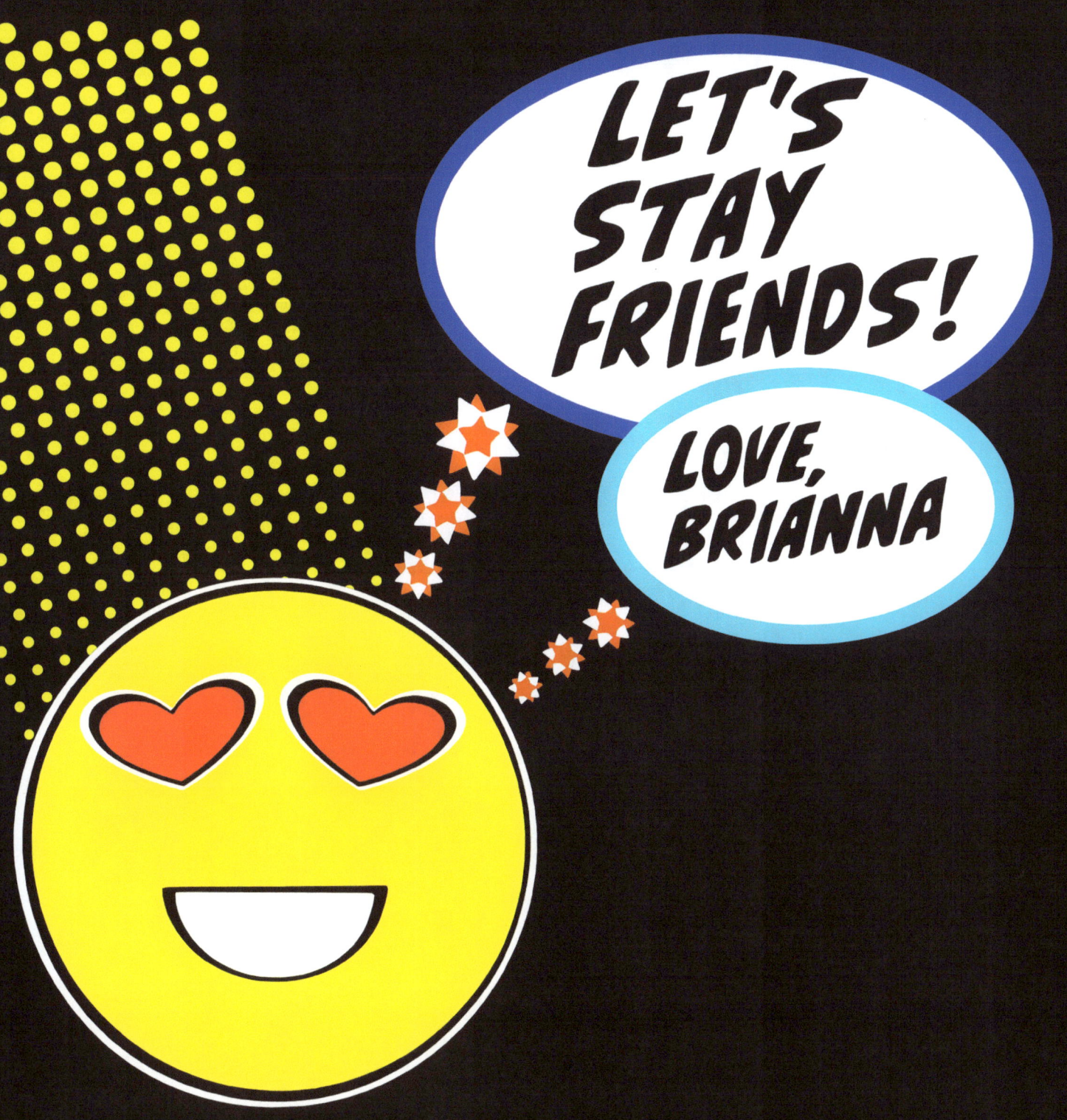

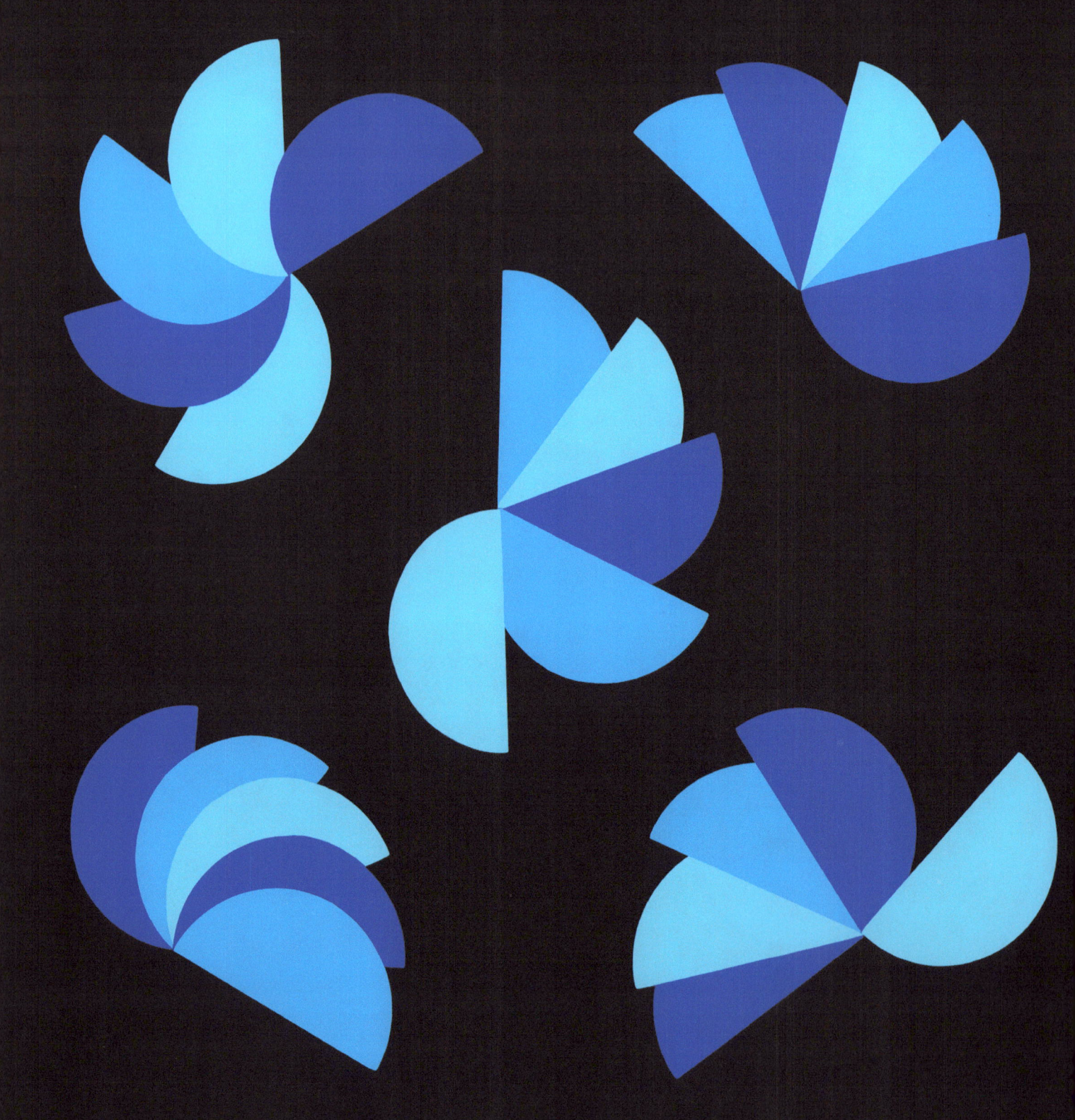

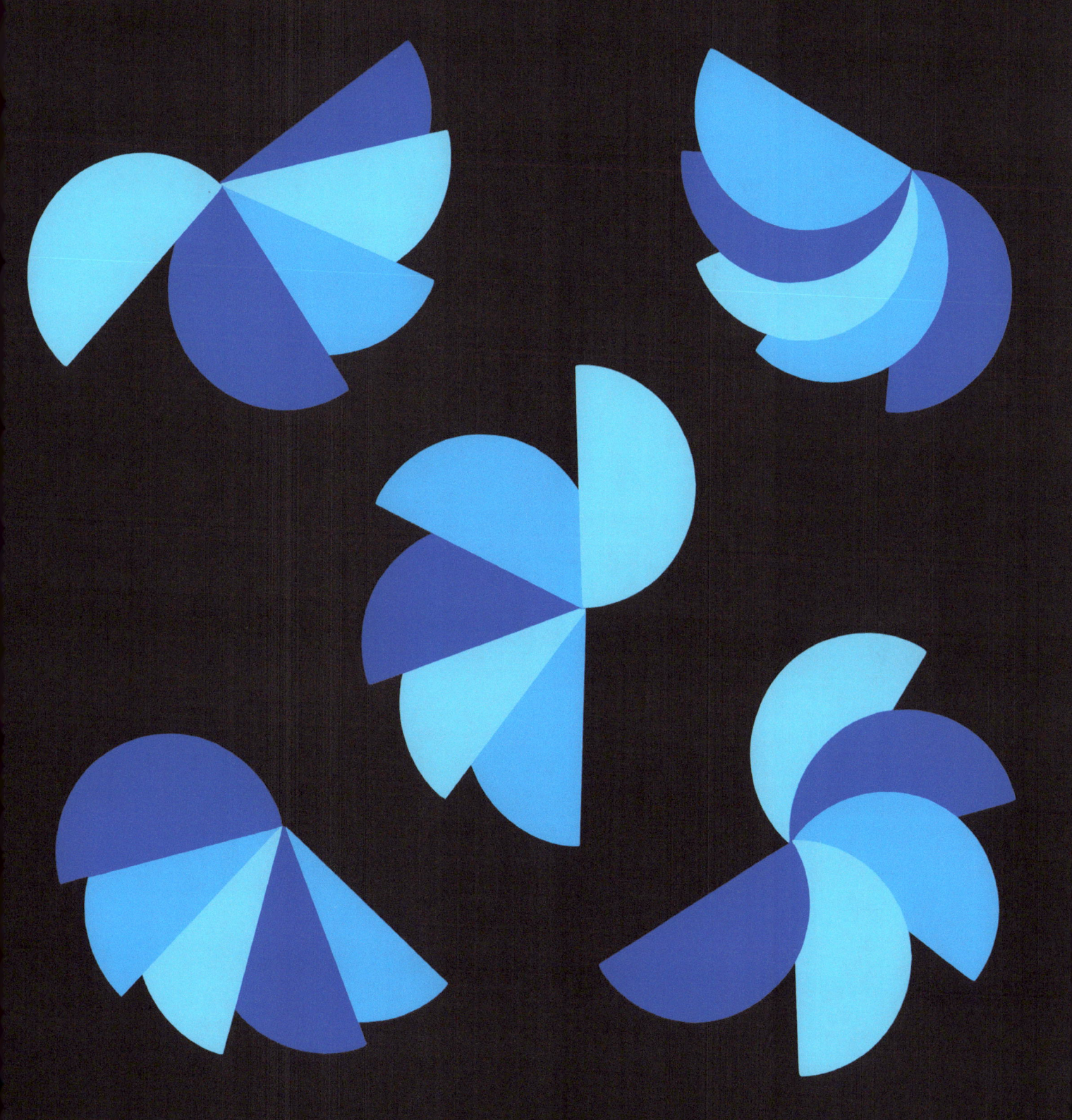

POP ART BOOKs
AVAILABLE NOW

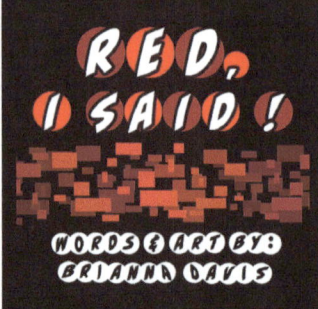
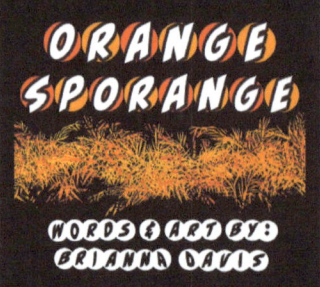
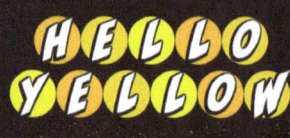
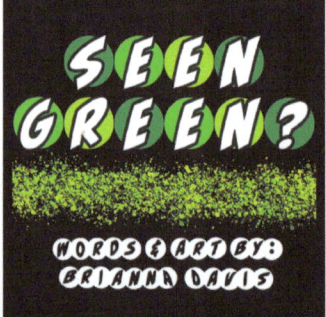
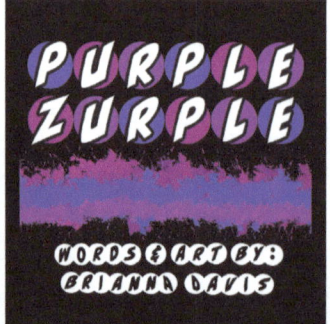
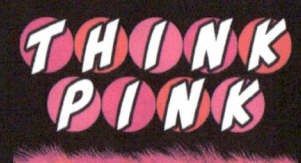
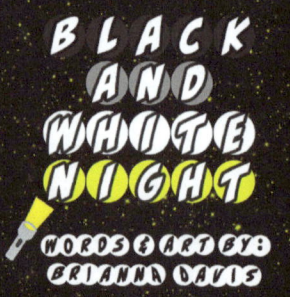
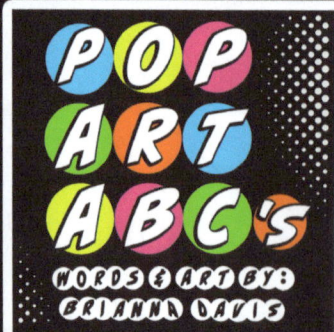
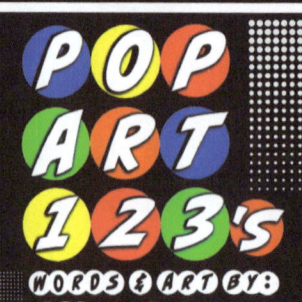

- Red, I Said! — Words & Art by: Brianna Davis
- Orange Sporange — Words & Art by: Brianna Davis
- Hello Yellow — Words & Art by: Brianna Davis
- Seen Green? — Words & Art by: Brianna Davis
- Purple Zurple — Words & Art by: Brianna Davis
- Think Pink — Words & Art by: Brianna Davis
- Black and White Night — Words & Art by: Brianna Davis
- Pop Art ABC's — Words & Art by: Brianna Davis
- Pop Art 123's — Words & Art by: Brianna Davis

www.ingramcontent.com/pod-product-compliance
Lightning Source LLC
Chambersburg PA
CBHW051828210526
45473CB00005B/1791